Penultimata

Penultimata

Robert Conquest

WAYWISER

First published in 2009 by

THE WAYWISER PRESS

14 Lyncroft Gardens, Ewell, Surrey KT17 1UR, UK
P.O. Box 6205, Baltimore, MD 21206, USA
www.waywiser-press.com

Managing Editor
Philip Hoy

Associate Editors
Joseph Harrison   Clive Watkins   Greg Williamson

A CIP catalogue record for this book is available from the British Library

ISBN 978-1-904130-36-9

Printed and bound by
Cromwell Press Group, Trowbridge, Wiltshire

*for John Gross and Sam Gwynn
defenders of the faith*

Acknowledgements

Acknowledgements are above all due to the skill and energy shown by R. S. Gwynn – poet, critic, and fine example – in organising this collection. Some of these poems first appeared in the *London Magazine*, the *Times Literary Supplement*, *Encounter*, the *New Statesman*, *The Spectator*, *The Listener*, *Hellas*, *The Formalist*, the *American Spectator*, the *Poetry Society Christmas Supplement*, the *New Criterion*, *The Guardian*, the *Los Angeles Times*, the *Dragons of Expectation*, *The Liberal*, *First Things*, *Standpoint* and elsewhere.

Contents

I

II

Contents

III

IV

Contents

I

Ignition

Perhaps a bird-call
No different from hundreds heard
In life, and the bird
Not clearly identifiable,

Or a high-stepping girl
Crossing a plank-bridge
Into focus rather than knowledge
Into accept rather than feel,

A seed, a sigh, a scrawl
On the back of an envelope
To attain a full shape
Later, if at all.

In Attendance

The small park, May, calm moment in their wooing.
On the face of it everything's theirs:
Pear-blossom only half conceals
Faint haze round the Western hills
Clear blue above southward spires,
Over town-murmur uninsistent cooing
As the touch of a warm breeze
All but skirt-liftingly moves
Across the rose-gold of her thighs
And ruffles the appropriate doves.

Doves? But there's something wrong. Their gait
Jerky, piston-like, a tick-tock
Inconclusive strut, male after mate,
Puffed-out plumage, ill-tempered look,
For all one knows lice-ridden ... Hardly part of
Aphrodite's train. Nor like some great
Artist's sky-projected Descent of the Dove
As the extreme white wingspread of a religion's
High point. The less satisfactory type of bird
Among these flower-beds can only rate
A less emotive, more objective word.
– So make it pigeons.

But perhaps, or even certainly,
We cannot quite break the cypher
That links mood to reality.
If this breeze is not the Cyprian zephyr
Nor this sky the nest of the white numen,
Their own mutuality must transcend
Even their own imperfect selves.
She is as much goddess as any woman,
And their own warm day dissolves
All attributes other than love's.

Grey-blue feathers glow, bird-voices blend,
Let's call them doves.

Two Occasions

1. Beached

A sweep of greener-than-azure sea and
A stretch of paler-than-gold sand
Hemmed in by shore-shadowing pines
From under which, just out of the sun
He looks down at a supine woman
Shapely, even beautiful, but one
On whom he has no designs.
Her bikini, taut between thigh and curved abdomen,
Shows soft fronds of her
Dark intercrural fur.
And he's suddenly overcome by an access
Of tenderness.

2. Heard Melodies

Moment, and then memory
May be stamped deep with a dreamsight
Some faint sound reifies,
As when tides of night run high
Round lifting breasts and thighs:

On a girl lit faintly by
Curtain-muffled moonlight
Love breaks like a wave, then dies;
And she gives a little cry
Or a series of little cries.

Only Natural

A huge moon sits on the reef.
Half-aware, he turns away from
Its power inland down from the cliff-path
towards her parents' home

Descending out of the direct
Beam on the track through the treed slope.
It's not even that they reject
Him. Too young: but they don't know how deep,

How far ... And now, half a world
Away, their sudden posting will take
Her at just the moment the love-meld
Has not yet set firm. Will it break

Or hold? In this early hour
Of the second night that should have been
Theirs, he moves under cypress, cedar,
Their high leafages ungreen

In the cool lunar ashlight's white-gold
Glow, perfused from the parallel
Sweep down on his face's controlled
Expression at the doorway. He sounds the bell.

2

Now he prepares to endure
The night that should have been theirs.
Her father comes beaming to the door.
And she's behind him on the stairs:

A smile's quick complicity. Her
Hair, her ear-rings so set out that oval
Absolute ... He pulls himself together
As her mother, too, vaguely greets his arrival.

Tonight was to have been theirs
Like last week's stolen, complete
Modulation of thirty-six hours,
The days fruitful as the night.

He can't blame them celebrating
The new job overseas. And she'll
Be back in late spring.
More guests. In to dinner. They file

Under the motile glitter
Of chandeliers, in a warm
Welcoming familial chatter,
The same bracelet on her bare arm ...

How can he stand this? She's the far side
Of the table, two down. Why can't those
Others see that they're all black-and-white
While she's in full colour, jade, gold, rose?

She leans forward, managing to say
Across the grapeglow-filled glasses,
"Never mind – I'll be back in May,"
Spoken without any emphasis.

Then her eyes brush his lightly like the thin
Electric thread that precedes
And guides the lightning, in
This case broken off ... He needs

To think in different terms. Reality
Is around them like barbed fences
And for now he has to remain physically
Passive inside his senses.

And these have sharpened – even taste:
The smoked salmon, the delicate
Moselle, and after that the roast
Duck, the burgundy, beset his palate.

The fruit, the port. Eventually
It's over. Cheeks just kissed
Formally, he hopes feelingly.
Then he's free and unfree at last.

3

Outside. The moon's gone: but his
Sight after a few moments adjusts
To the underbrush's intricacies
Of shade, the high overcast's

Smooth smudged charcoal, the upflung
Foliate antennae edging more sharply
Their arched life form, as he treads along
Its track to the cliff-top, to descry

The northern ness's distant chalk-face
Now an almost livid non-pallor,
And West the sleek panther-black sea's
Slow pulse. He's hurt. But the phenomena

Distract, if not quite soothe, the way
They seem to command acceptance of his place
In this random, uncompelled display
Of different darknesses.

On the Veranda

"The girl-losing experience ..."
His voice stirred up the soft silence
Where, sundowners in hand, the men's

Attention – mutual, serene, content –
Was over the warm, quiescent
Sea, under a dark blue firmament

With brush-stroke mistiness out westerly
As the good sunglow resumed slowly
Into the waters. A touch of melancholy

Imbued the ambience like a dash
Of angostura. "A longish
Time since that sort of anguish

Hit me. She was my very first.
She left me for one older, more self-possessed,
Richer – sure! – better-dressed.

– I was only a scruffy, last term
Student. Much later she told me what scum,
What a swine, he'd been. – Well, some

Consolation. Not enough to reverse
The long loss, the intolerable years
Of – I expect much the same as yours."

"Mine perhaps worse, since all my own fault.
Divorced, I thought that I'd play the field
With two girls, often three. I felt

Safe from the love-trap. Then one day
No. 1 switched to a fiancé.
Part of the deal – you'll rightly say

A miscalculation – I've learned better since.
The nights! I'd take four or five aspirins
With large shots of bourbon in half pints

Of milk, drunk quick to stop curdling, slept
If at all, with my right big and second toes kept
(With no erotic feeling) round my left

Achilles tendon. – I mention this
So that we wouldn't perhaps miss
Any pointer to full diagnosis."

"Sleep, yes. And drink. This smooth rum
Recalls how, when her bad letter came,
Stationed in Orkney, I couldn't get warm.

Before, I'd not minded the scything cold
But now four blankets – and rum – left me chilled.
– Another symptom of getting ungirled?"

"Well, here's a memory I'd quite long striven
To repress. We'd been married more than eleven
Years. All was dull – was depressing, even.

No adultery on either side.
Wanting more operas, cruises, she'd
Left from a boredom I thought I'd shared.

But in the event, the parting tore
As jagged, as barbed as any before
When young. A wound that for long stayed raw ..."

Turning now from the sea and sun
A drier voice, "Well, my contribution
To, I suppose, this panel discussion,

Since I imagine that between you
You've covered every important issue ..."
He paused for a sip, "here's a minor clue:

I had made love to her just twice,
The bond hadn't clamped down like a vice.
Then she went back to her rather nice

Chap. At the wheel on the Brompton Road
My tear-ducts all of a sudden flowed.
The traffic light was luckily red.

Yes, a close escape, which may illustrate
The problems posed." "What we still await
Is how, and why, can our psyches get

Gripped till almost as fused as steel?
There's surely no good biological
Reason?" "An unfavourable

Mutation?" ...
                    "What have we exorcized?
In each mind-vault now perhaps a weaker ghost
Walled up, but not quite put to rest?"

– A last strongish drink then, toasting the bronze
Sunset and the warm, gentle ocean's
Uneasy effacement of demons.

Beyond Them

"*Perfect*'s a word you mustn't use",
She said (softly, strongly)
That evening after the long fuse
Of their love had finally

Brought shattering release
Of their imaginings into reality,
And with it, like all realities,
Some imperfection, incongruity ...

Well: out in bright cirrus-sifted noon
Drenched by a sudden shower-spray;
At lunch her brief choke on a fish-bone,
Rather too sharp a Chardonnay.

Even bodily, the odd glitch
In their so overdue rites of union ...
Still, little more than snags in the rich
Damascene of that attuning;

Like the one distracting flaw
In an old Persian's carpet-weaving
To appease what he saw
As the envious eyes of heaven.

But she'd chosen the wrong moment.
Lying, with her head on her right hand,
Her eyes livelily, lazily, intent
On where he happened to stand

(About eight o'clock from the end of the bed,
Some five feet distant). For through her smile's
Full calm there glowed, quick, unexpected,
A coherence of irrefutables.

Not just her cream-bronze candor displayed
On the coverlet's cream-citron
Chenille as early eventide
Gently shone through the soft curtain.

Not just the high, hand-filling breasts,
Or vision sweeping the tactility of
The smooth, hand-soothing thigh-and-waist's
Concord of curves. Not even love.

More as if a great painter (Venetian
School?) had stood and sought
With a life-trained concentration,
Grip of genius, toil of thought

To fix the exact point, the fulcrum
To raise beauty-scatter, love-breath
Up out of the natural world, to some
Cool altitude of truth

Which would, he already knew, lie clear
Unfailingly, unfadingly engraved
In the scan of his mind's eye, year after year.
And so it proved.

Looking Up

How have things changed since Romeo
Sang under Juliet's
Window of opportunity?

When you're so much older
And have been so often exposed
You might develop immunity ...

Light, lighter than snow
Falls on the Savernake
And streams down the upper Stour

As she too leans from a window
Of a friend's context of cottage
Through thatch matching her hair

Undeniably evoking
Verona and that moon-viewed
Honey-voiced Capulet

Visioned through years and distances
And heard now above the high
Thrum of a west-winging jet ...

Anniversary

How should I write it?
How not to sound mawkish
When thanking a wife for
Another good year? How
To set up a trophy
Or cut a new notch in
The tally of gladness?

Images? Well, then,
I see you this summer:
Sunrise and sunset
(We *did* see the sun rise?)
Then a great moon to southward
Air heavy with fuchsia,
Driving and loving,
Swimming and dreaming ...

As for your faults, well
The way that you sometimes ...
But I'd better not spoil it.
Just the same when ... however
We won't let the public
In on such wrangles
And it's wholly forgiven
(It's even forgiven
That you forgave me):
The merest of jolts on
The smooth-swinging freeway
On the drive to wherever.

Once or twice seeing
At dawn with you sleeping
Your face on the pillow ...
But watch it! I'm getting

A bit sentimental.
I'll tell you in private.

What a year, what a life! I'll
Just close by moving
A vote of thanks – carried
Without opposition.
And now we'll move on to
Next year's agenda
(Where 'more of the same' will
Be strongly supported.)

Afterwards

'recollected in tranquillity'

Is it so necessary
For a wild memory
To fade and blur
Before the full charge
Of an old love or rage
Can really register?

With a life's long perspectives
The changed picture gives
More depth and scope
As twisted faces shrink
To little more than pink
Blobs on its landscape ...

A passion, sharp and hot,
Might once have seized the heart
To rip or scald.
So far as this can be
Recalled in tranquillity
It's not recalled.

The Last Day (Embarkation Leave)

Squeezing the water from bright braids
She stumbles, almost gracefully, towards him
Up the steep grass of the cove's brim
To their alcove under the colonnade's

White and westward curve to the ford's
Almost awash stepping-stones
Among a scattered flush of rhododendrons ...
She smiles. Her towel clings. And he hoards

This among other images: asleep on the sand;
Doing a little jig at a bus-stop;
Quiet in half-dark with a wine-cup
Nursed in both palms; and; and; and.

2

Dry now, suffused, mutual, they sit:
A time of slow knowledge, as last
Night was a time of precipitate trust.
And so the wide gaze opens to admit

The deep view, deep as their mood: soft airs;
Comforting waters; calm light – except
Where frayed fronds of a thin cataract
At the cove's head scatter small flares;

Salt-scent; thyme-tang; transsensual skies.
And it's not that the outspread scene
Is no more than props for their stage, the sun
Its arc-lamp. But it amplifies.

3

They aren't alone. There are others who murmur
Or stroll at the edge of their felt range.
But that's not why they exchange
No more than a few looks, and fewer

Words, in the mere now, the extreme now,
Where love sustains the near-silence
As our furthest, profoundest ocean's
Swell might lift a proa's prow.

And it's not that particles of a shared air
Drift away gently from one's lungs
Into the other's, over tongues
Which have touched. It's more

That what surrounds them seems to be
A stress-fluid, a field of force
With gentle but diamond-forging pressures.
Mind-sparklings leap from the quantum-sea ...

And the day dwindles. But still love
Glows through the globe's turning
An unappeasable yearning
For what they already have.

4

Evening smoothes out every surface
Of water, of vision. The low sun's
Presence strikes up to them bronze
From the hard refracting grasses.

Above which a flight of doves
Having banked and twice circled
Is absorbed into the flickering dark-gold
Dome of a sycamore. Mauves,

Magentas, dim down. They must leave, not just loving
But even more fearing, into the imminent
Death-fogs, where today may have meant
What? Everything? Nothing?

They rise. Some quality of the late light
Takes the edge off the squared
Stonework of the crossing. Muffled cloud
Vaguely pervades. The moments concentrate

And confuse. And a low blue demilune
Is all that's left of the sky as from the day's
Depth they take their separate ways
– To merge again? Not certainly. Not soon.

Lost Love

'The climate of the heart'? – Young men
Who think they won't survive it when
That organ takes the icy blast
May find that once the winter's past
Their blood's been only slightly thinned
By the unprevailing wind.

II

Phryne

"It's such a pity that we don't have
Anything like a photograph
Of her about whom the ancients rave ..."

He'd been talking about the well-known tale
Of her lawyer at her blasphemy trial
Baring her breasts to gain an acquittal.

Now, it wasn't the 'beauty' of what they saw
That made the judges unloop the law,
But what's been described as 'sacred awe'.

Would visual be better than verbal, though,
Projected into the long-ago
Till we think we know what we'll never know?

Fragments, copies, museums still hold
Of statues she modeled, or so we're told
(Though not the Delphi one in gold).

Well, at Thespiae how did they feel as
Praxiteles, daring celestial malice,
Set up together, on equal pillars

Statues of her and of Aphrodite.
A girl and a Goddess damn-near Almighty
With a temper not to be taken lightly?

He could only pre-empt their sacred fear
With what could unarguably appear
As spillover from another sphere

On to physique made partly free
From the pressures of externality
Which is all that the subtlest lens can see.

(And Marilyns, Sophias, the very cream
Of our time, aren't sewn without a seam
Directly into the fabric of dream.)

But she's gone! Long gone! Gone to the grave
And left us, instead of a photograph,
The residual glow of an ancient grief.

In Both Senses

Scarcely discernible at first
Faint peachlight spills through blinds undrawn:
A soft susurrus from the East
Gently proclaiming dawn.

The sun, a single cymbal still
Ringing from some cosmic beat ...
Noon's loud light that seems to fill
Our minds with throbs of heat.

The red-brown dusk bays like a hound
That greets its master's late return:
That is, translated out of sound,
Kind warmths that do not burn.

Then Leonids streak across the sky
Without a whisper ... Frozen tears,
High deeps, with senses tightened by
The muteness of the spheres.

Deep Down

Guides to a City church (All Hallows) note
Dug up from Roman levels of the crypt
'Fragments of a figurine of Venus.'

How young the city was then. Not so long
Since Virgil had recited to Maecenas
Those lines on 'Britain from the world cut off.'

One's first thought is, how far into our past,
The sixty generations laid between us
In clay-borne sites to which the mana clings

Imprints in twisted strata grinding down:
Cracked tepidarium tiles, a copper bowl's
Merest outline oxidized to greenness,

Flakes of crushed plaster, chips of paving-stone,
Grains of sand perhaps blown from the arena's
Killing floor some half a mile away.

– It was a violent age, a brutal age:
Seen too in smeared black streaks from the Iceni's
Burning of London (61 AD.)

2

How could this cool and gentle image then
Make headway in the presence of a queen as
Ruthless, and as wronged, as Boadicea?

Or with such other claims to goddesshood
As all those pompous busts and bas-reliefs,
Deified tarts, Poppaeas and Faustinas?

And then Priapus, not so much obscene as
Coarse, crude, with phalli cut in street or wall
As signposts to some squalid lupanar.

Yet skill and sentiment carved out this calm
Recruit to Aphrodite and Athene's
Alliance against manic, smouldering lusts

– Though, shaped and smoothed, the young divinity
Is physical in presence, and the vulva's
Delicate notch does not debar the penis,

Giving Pandemian and Uranian love
Conjoined as with the writhing amphisbaena's
Two heads – transcendent dark, transcendent light.

3

But more immediately, this figurine is
(Something about the thighs) as if dug up
From strata of memory, a personal past

Distorted, crumbled, shifted in the mind
Out of that year when they were both nineteen, his
Life a daze of flared limbs, starspun hair.

A quiet kiss beside a Cotswold mere
In the erotic's earliest novenas
Eyes focussed far beyond the possible.

Muffled with rugs against the salt wind's keenness
Side by side on a ship's upper deck
Warmly together, half-asleep, content.

Yelling a chorus in a rowdy bar
Somewhere off the Rue des Feuillantines, as
Bright-eyed, red-cheeked as a female clown.

Pub bedroom, Kent: slipping from crêpe-de-chine as
Sleek as the figure now displayed in all
The reginality of Renoir's girls.

And not much else. Distanced, displaced, diminished,
What's left of love and beauty just survives
Like fragments of that figurine of Venus.

Goethe in 1816

Sunlight breaks dazzling from the stream
    But he is not deceived,
Nor when the young breeze shakes that gleam
    From trees gone golden-leaved.

But as he turns, with eyes undimmed
    To watch that warm sun sink,
A young shape, deep-eyed, golden-limbed
    Stands poised upon a brink.

Declension into saint or sage
    Is not worth thinking of:
Into the cold pool of his age
    She dives and brings up love.

The Idea of Virginia

It lay in the minds of poets: coasts fronting Arcadias
Sprang from the parchment map Doctor Dee in his study
Scanned for likely lodes of Philosopher's Stone.
But the land was also real: rivers, meads, mountains.

Deer and pumas ranged its high plains. Beavers
Toiled in its streams. Bluebird and mocking-bird,
Blue jay, redbird and quail filled branches and air.
In its woods poplar, walnut, cedar, mulberry grew green

Round glades clear of all undergrowth but the grape.
The dogwood blossomed in white clusters, the judas tree
In purplish buds. Clumps of sassafras, sumac, persimmon
Variegated the lush savannahs. From swamps

Rose up the sharp scent of the bog-magnolia.
Overhead, miles of canvasbacks arrowed the Chesapeake.
The runs were full of trout, shad, sheepshead, the bays
Of oysters. And among this abundance were men.

In spring they ate turkey and hare; in summer venison,
Terrapin, oysters on dry leaves, strawberries;
In winter tuckahoe, fish on fire sticks, hominy.
They drank a brew of hickory nuts. They smoked tobacco.

In his wooden palace in Werowocomoco,
His vassal werowances round him, Powhatan sat.
At each comer loomed a terrible image in wood:
A dragon, a bear, a puma; the last was a man.

The barbarian emperor had fled his faraway clan;
Hacked out a realm, seen two generations die.
No Atahualpa or Montezuma in gold-clogged pomp,
He had strength, subtlety and a few thousand braves.

He wore a grey raccoon fur. His wives moved in mantles
Of bluebird feathers, or heron or swan, embroidered
With animal figures. He lived in his treasure of weapons
And his two daughters: the elder was Pocahontas.

– And so great spaces, feelings, fruitfulnesses poured
Their warm potentials over a fallow landscape.
Its other affluent brimmed in a far-off island:
Liberties, laws, the strong consensual state.

2

As the *Susan Constant* approached the Capes, even before
The pine-tops of the low coast pricked the horizon,
The smell of the land came from behind the sand-dunes,
Blown from the miles of forest, the flower-pied grasses.

They built their Jamestown, triangular, wooden-walled,
On a fevered island – for protection from Spain,
With skimped corn-fields – not to hide Indian scouts;
A miserable lot, they would have starved amidst plenty.

But among them a secret strength, the conquistador
For this goldless small land was ready – John Smith,
The man of no birth and no name, a century after
The spear-proud Spaniards awarded his king no empire

But a few thousand acres where a few hundred English
Could scarcely hold. Yet was as strong, as subtle
A village Cortez as Powhatan, his friend, his rival,
Surpassed in cunning the lords of the treasure realms.

He had fought in France, Holland; thrown overboard as heretic;
A privateer; a soldier in Transylvania;
His own pike felling the three Turks' heads of his arms;
Captured, enslaved, killing his Pasha, escaping.

Now seized by Powhatan, his head on a stone
To be brained by tomahawks, but Pocahontas springing
Between – if the tale be true, and even if true
The rescue not a charade of Powhatan's guile.

He saw her again. On some mission to Werowocomoco
He and his men sat by their fire in a meadow.
Pocahontas slipped from the woods with thirty maidens,
Leaves on her thighs, an otter-skin round her waist,

The horns of a deer on her head. She carried a bow.
A quiver hung on her back. Her skin was painted;
Her companions' too, each in a different colour.
They circled in an impersonal, passionate dance.

They chanted, but did not speak. They ran to the woods.
He did not see her again till she slipped to his camp
To warn of threatened attack. "Next to God, the instrument,"
He wrote, to save them all from famine and slaughter.

3

When he went the colony crumbled. Dale saved it.
Amid riots, hunger, false reports to London,
Conspiracies to assassinate the Governor. Yet,
"If you give over this country and lose it," he wrote,

"You with your wisdom will leap such a gudgeon
As our state has not done the like since we lost the Kingdom
Of France. I have seen the best countries in Europe ...
Put them all together this will be the equivalent unto them

If it be inhabited by good people." They came, good and bad.
The Assembly's Speaker was Pozy, late MP at Westminster.
The same year the first black slave was sold by a Dutchman.
Settlers trickled in, and women: the poor and ignorant,

The rich and inquisitive, Sandys, poet and traveller,
Wyatt, the old poet's grandson. Plantations spilled westward.
Powhatan died: his heirs launched massacre twice,
But it was too late. The indentured servants arrived,

And, from the war in England, the younger sons
Of the defeated faction, ensigns of Rupert's Horse,
Of the Bluecoats of Naseby. Two new styles of toughness.
– And the first generation too of the native born.

All sought liberty, word of so many meanings.
All recognized, however reluctantly, law.
Freedom was a fresh breeze down from the Blue Ridge Mountains;
Slavery a stench up from the Great Dismal Swamp.

So through the varying centuries the land lived on,
Flawed in the stone of its cracked foundation, frayed
By the quotidian wear of the generations;
Its Form flickered and faded: but never died.

And the frontier rolled inland, Tidewater to Piedmont,
Piedmont to Shenandoah. Spotswood, sounding the passes,
Gave small golden horseshoes to all his companions
Richly engraved, "Sic juvat transcendere montes."

And in the townless miles the great houses glowed.
Self-confidence; trade and toil; duelling and horses;
The frontier code honed the aristocratic code.
A legendary generation approached its moment.

4

Haydn, prose, elections, deism, architecture,
Bred the leaders of battle, governance, law.
Washington, Marshall, Madison, Jefferson, Henry
Defended a heightened England from an England lapsed.

In a capitol later modelled on the Maison Carrée
The orators talked down tyranny. Fifty miles away
Their general accepted the English commander's sword.
– But then the new state grew stagnant, its fresh colour fading.

And the next efflorescence was war. All the red scars of
The Bloody Angle, the Crater, a hundred battles.
Great regiments faded on Cemetery Ridge;
Great captains lay crushed by the heavier guns.

With the best of the young men dead, the country ruined,
And the sourness of Military District no. 1,
The War was an after-image, a dominant lightning
To dazzle the stunned eyes of a generation.

But Lee in his college office in Lexington,
The man beyond criticism, spoke reconciliation.
Slavery at least was gone. Over yet one more century
As the wounds heal up, the flaws start slowly to fade.

The dogwood blooms, the cardinals perch, the lean hounds hunt
Where Pocahontas danced, where John Smith scouted, where
    Spotswood rode,
Where Washington marched to victory, Jackson to death,
By the slow rivers, the cool woods, the mountains, the marshes.

The Idea, never fulfilled, was never abandoned;
The free order only approaches its goal.
The land lived on imperfect in city and forest,
Its Form half-remembered; as it lay in the minds of poets.

Placerville

(California mining country)

After the temblor the strata settle
What was gold-dust in a slowing stream
Falls from that suspended gleam
Into solidities of lode-metal.

Shock, aftershock – over in days,
Consolidation of gold – eons:
But on our conceptual screens
Time knows its place.

In ten minutes a couple buy
At the store where such are sold
A ring struck from that gold
Engraved Eternity.

Below the Belt

In an essay on seaside postcards Orwell
Found one was 'obscene' without being 'immoral'
– Inciting to nothing that's extramarital.

Broad bawdy, of course, cannot quite claim
Such fine amenity as its aim,
Yet it does seek to warm, and not to inflame.

Laugh-shaken, relaxed, subversive, a taste
Brewed up from humanity's seething yeast.
For some, that appetite's sadly decreased.

– Your seven-legged octopus may survive
(perhaps only six-legged, even five)
Not fully operational, half-alive.

So spare us the frigid, 'transgressive' sorts
Of obscenity, with po-faced graduates
Jargoning away like juggernauts

Bargaining away ... and we're rotten-ripe
With comics replacing mothers-in-law, tripe,
With a tedious tart-and-genitals hype.

To be fair, one must distinguish that from
The steaming Rugger Club's sonic boom,
The snigger of the Senior Common Room.

And the eighty verses of Kirriemuir
May not be rated as literature,
But still, their tone overlaps with the truer

Craft of the limerick, a serious game,
Wild fantasy, taut epigram,
Polished and cut like a five-line gem

Plucking the sensuous and mental strings
Giving the rhythmic structure wings
To stir up the psyche's happenings.

2

They say women wince trying not to envision
Every organ, act or emission
While men just enjoy the verbal sedition.

That delicacy must be fairly addressed
(Though many exceptions might be pressed:
The Wives of Windsor and Bath, Mae West).

Still the genre seems somehow to correspond
To what they say about how men bond
The mâle gaieté, si triste et profonde

De Musset noted – and while we're abroad
There's Pushkin's shameless Gavriliad,
Voltaire's Pucelle, – and a gasconade

Of 'Gallic salt' songs: (Bishop Dupanloup
Won immortality – though it's true
Not the sort that he had in view).

Well, back in England, from Chaucer on
In public (and privately Tennyson)
With Shakespeare, as ever, standing alone.

He 'shocked' ? – Not with sex. For that he'd use fright, as
With, perhaps, a bunch of first-nighters
Taking a drink between acts of Titus

Andronicus, and hearing the management's
Calling out to the audience
"We're expecting a little turbulence

Please return to your seats." Then the theatre's
Dead silence. – But with Hamlet's country matters
Their guffawed complicity shook the rafters.

Coarse tastes he reluctantly drifted with?
 – That has long since been exposed as myth
For instance by Logan Pearsall Smith

Who makes it clear that a lot of his double
Meanings could only be caught by the subtle
Wit-epicures of the Mermaid circle.

Critics also note his obscenity
Exceeding other rhymesters' in quantity
 – A side effect of genius and sanity?

So one hardly needs great scholarly probes
To show that, his patience being less than Job's,
He'd have said that the prigs and the anthrophobes

Were bit-players talking a lot of Globes.

Campania

"One party among us made the ascent of Vesuvius, while others preferred the fertile valley (source of the famed wines of the area). P., however, chose neither, visiting instead the barren region north-west of Naples, known mainly for its repulsive character. V., in his dry way, suggested that this reflected P's taste in artistic matters ..." – *A Travel Diary, 1887*

The Arts that seriously address
The raising of the consciousness
Bloom in a spread of themes and tones
– Geology of various zones.

Some scale the great volcano – sky,
Flame, precipice, immensity.
While some tread, in the charming vale,
The villages-and-vineyards trail.

The grandeur group (though kindly) tends
To mock at its more modest friends,
While they, in turn, are quick to spot
Pretensions in the peak-proud lot.

But both despise one who resigns
The glorious vistas, the green vines,
For Phlegrean Fields that gall each sense
With flat glooms round mephitic vents.

A matter of tastes and temperaments.

At the Rebirth of St Petersburg

White nights of the northern city,
Blue eyes of one of its women.
Light brims up over the Pole, limning
With surfaces of serenity

Gold spires, green squares, grey river
Where today's dusk is tomorrow's dawn.
Sheets of light under the swansdown
Sky sweep through, around, over,

Unsilting every dulled sense,
Flexing every frozen mood
Of the stranger from a lower latitude.
Peeling from lulled waters, sky-silence,

How can such fineness run so rich?
– Laminations of light, ermine, almond,
Dissolved into the wholly transparent:
A fluid purity to leach

Out the crass, the quotidian,
Mind blanched to take stronger hues
And above all her eyes'. That blue's
Even more confirmatory than

All those wide-winged whitenesses:
With an unstinting radiance
Of acceptance, of endurance
Inexhaustible as the rich skies.

Profound plenitude, then:
Not the thin blue of the shallows,
– Unripe innocence that knows
Little of hate; nor like the alien

Flat amethyst ovals of sprites with
Snake-fascinations, snake-fears
In the cold springs, white-birch-hidden meres
Projected unfeeling from myth.

– And yet the inhuman has firmed
The depth and strength of that blue:
Here life's been indentured to
Troll, golem, the undead, the damned,

Mean fury has raved, ravenous
Down these streets, with claws of torture,
War, famine, lies, slaughter.
Terror-hammer, falsehood-furnace

Crushed the selfish, or just weak, to mere
Clinker, to twisted scrap; but
The fine, the firm, with eyes half-shut
Was forged through years in that fire

To a gentle strength, to a charm
Against all that's false and cruel:
And that blue is the sheen of a steel
It took white heats to anneal.

But now the white night is cool,
The eyes upon mine are calm.

In Place

Six Malverns cluster round the hills
From Malvern Link to Malvern Wells
    Great, Little, North and West,
And, high above the ridge upthrown
From North Hill down to Raggedstone
    The Beacon's windy crest.

Where Langland, as our language woke,
Saw a fair field full of folk
    Past Teme and Evesham vales,
Where Auden like an admiral stood
On the old rocks, from which he could
    Scan storm-clouds over Wales.

Where back in the Armada's days
"Twelve fair counties saw the blaze
    From Malvern's lonely height",
My grandfather would say thirteen.
The toposcope which shows the scene
    Appears to prove him right.

The Assembly Rooms: those summer days
Of Festival – its concerts, plays,
    The strange crowd it would draw:
One incident I well recall:
My sister on her bicycle
    Knocked down George Bernard Shaw.

High, dominating, half way down
The slope of the steep-streeted town,
    The Priory's grey mass.
Its old font I was christened at
And outside, by a buttress that
    Shaded their patch of grass,

Some wooden crosses from the War
With aluminium strips that bore
      Both my uncles' names.
The younger with the Worcesters fell
Aged nineteen at Passchendaele –
      The shadow nothing tames

Deep in our elders' eyes still hung
But never thrust upon the young
      Though sometimes, nothing said,
A look that seemed to scan one's face
As though one could in part replace
      The irreplaceable dead ...

The ghastly prep-school where I went
And all those winters that we spent
      With chilblains or with flu
(Or both). And where a gross cuisine
Of gristle stewed in margarine
      Sustained us as we grew.

The little Malvern House Hotel
Where I was born, and St. Anne's Well
      Among its elms and firs.
The bookshop off the Promenade
In which the choice was sometimes hard
      – Astounding or New Verse.

And so we felt our minds expand.
Not only that, as when the band
      Played at the Hydro Ball.
Paul Jones starts. With luck one wins
Esme or Pam, the lovely twins,
      Or Wendy, best of all.

Memories clear up like mist:
The second girl I ever kissed
   (The first was out in Wales)
The very first whose breasts I bared
– But on the sentiments we shared
   Is where description fails ...

A sweet tryst by the British Camp
– Strange interweave of ditch and ramp:
   What if such history's died?
Or if, as that old poet sings,
"We shall not see the holy kings
   Ride down by Severn side."

For yet at Powick by the Teme
We'd meet; or down on Severn stream
   In gun emplacements for
The final fighting and the worst,
As Powick skirmish was the first,
   In England's Civil War ...

Back to the Beacon: to the East
There is no higher ground at least
   Until some Ural peak.
The wind off all of Europe's ice
Scrubbed clear the granite and the gneiss.
   We hugged, too cold to speak ...

– Some of the fragments that I shored
Against my going off abroad
   When I had turned eighteen.
And looking back across the years
I hardly think it all coheres
   Nor grasp all it may mean.

Whenever

This age requires "a tongue that naked goes
Without more fuss than Dryden's or Defoe's."

Thus Wyndham Lewis – let me check – a long
Half century ago, in *One Way Song*.

Our age requires ... But first we should expound
What sort of age it is. Just look around!

An age that thinks it knows, what's known to none,
Just how societies and psyches run.

An age of terrorists and absolutes:
One primes the missile and the other shoots.

An age of intellectuals talking balls
Picked up in gutters or in lecture halls,

Illiterate nomads in their urban tents
And ideologies of virulence.

An age when creativity's essential
And people realize their full potential,

An age of people who're concerned, or care,
– With schemes that lead to slaughter everywhere.

An age of warheads and the KGB,
An age of pinheads and the Ph.D.

When churches pander to advanced regimes
Whose victims fill our nightmares with their screams,

Age that ignored the unavenged Ukraine
'Imperialist Britain' seething in its brain,

An age of art devised for instant shock
An age of aestheticians talking cock,

With education – but let's cool it, lads,
And say, a means of inculcating fads

For Loyalty's in bourgeois ethics set,
Taste a mere mirage we must all forget,

Judgement to Progress must incline its scales,
And Truth ensure that Prejudice prevails

Until, as Harry Harrison would say,
With us it's always Bowb-your-buddy Day.

– Suppose it is. Some think we need a verse
Disrupting the disruption ten times worse:

The vulpine howl; the ill-corrected proof;
The mumble from the mouth that lacks a roof;

Strumming a single toneless string will do,
Or else a mélange adultère de tout.

Well, plural decencies come down to this:
Our queasy tolerance extends to piss.

– Yet let our clarion of conclusion sound,
That, even more than Lewis's, we've found

Our age requires a tongue that naked goes
Without more fuss than Dryden's or Defoe's.

III

Demons Don't

Demons don't
                  trust anyone, anywhere. So on no account
Trust them yourself. If you have one pent
Safely (you think) in your pentacle, a faint
Steam rising from its coarse integument
Fixing you with its single yellow flint
Eye, apparently acquiescent,
Never relax for a single moment.
Across vast voids, your formula of constraint
Has brought it you, compelled not compliant
As the occasional twitch of its blunt
Black lobster-like claws may hint.
One crack in the diagram, one error in the chant
And in a howling strike you'll be sent
Spinning down the dark dimension-vortex river
To a terror of dreary torment.

Demons don't
                  laugh. That long crescent
Gash below the eye doesn't show enjoyment.
Nor do they weep – a mode of the plangent
Their solid-state physiologies prevent.
But they are glad, even briefly, to be absent
From their own sphere's stifling environment
And melancholy at their too imminent
Return there: flat, infinite in extent
Uniform but for the odd lava-drooling vent
Under a pallid, sagging firmament:
And the nullity – no event or incident
Except the occasional entrapment
Of a human victim – of which the whole point
For a while at least, is to relieve a
Tedium otherwise total, transcendent.

Demons don't
           love. And it's what they resent
Most, as an intolerable affront
To negation, when they detect the sentiment
In victims long exposed in the ambient
Horizonless, endless exhaustion-effluent.
In such, that is, as really repent
And not merely unwish, their arrogant
Distortings – from some of whom we've learnt
What we know of that realm: they are revenant
Because the realm regards even a remnant
Of that feeling as so indecent, so repugnant
That sometimes, cramped in a visceral, violent
Spasm, it hurls them back earthward. Gaunt,
Eyes clenched tight on both frost and fever,
They wander among us, saved but soul-burnt.

Demons don't
           die; hence the astonishment
They feel when faced with a quite frequent
Wish, which if they could they'd gladly grant.
Immortality may be what humans want
But knowing what it's like to live for ever
Demons don't.

I. M.

On this Memorial Day
I remember a basset hound:
Bluebell (such was her name)
Died on the first of May.
Her ashes lie in the ground
By the lawn where her favorite game,

Chase-your-master, was played
Through the warm afternoons.
Sweet-natured, stubborn, afraid
Only of wasps ... One of those
Almost unalloyed boons
That life sometimes bestows.

Uproarious welcomes! She'd streak
Down the hall, ears trailing with speed,
Her melodious bay ringing out;
She wouldn't lick, but she'd
Gently nuzzle your cheek,
Then escort you back through the flat.

Her voices: that bay, sweet and deep;
The long coyote-like peals
That Satchmo's horn would evoke;
A crescendo of make-believe growls
As she swaggered up with a stick;
Her contented sigh before sleep.

In the morning, when she awoke
After lazily taking note
Of your presence, she'd always roll
Over for you to stroke
The silky white hair of her throat.
Then off for our morning stroll.

Philip Larkin she knew as a friend
– The closest description of
The affable contact it was.
Every letter from him would end
"Greetings" or "regards" or "love
To Bluebell" ... It passed across

The small interspecies gap.
Once, out in Battersea Park,
He observed that, much unlike lots
Of dogs, even having a crap
Her back made a graceful arc,
Not one of your squalid squats.

A critic once said "Here's the deal:
You see her and old So-and-so
Being swept over a weir,
Which would you rescue?" "Her."
"Sentimentality!" "No,
That's when you fake what you feel."

Well, whether or not you agree,
She's gone as we all must go,
Comrade and comforter.
It's some consolation to know
I did my best for her,
She did her best for me.

On the move, she was always game.
She sturdily ploughed through the snows,
She lolled in the lukewarm meres,
She barked at two oceans ... Then those
Almost idyllic last years
Here in her final home.

I.M.

Whence she's gone as we all must go,
In her case leaving behind
A heartening afterglow,
A lasting awareness of
Those modulations of mind.
We lump together as love.

This Be the Worse

They fuck you up, the chaps you choose
To do your Letters and your Life.
They wait till all that's left of you's
A corpse in which to shove a knife.

How ghoulishly they grub among
Your years for stuff to shame and shock:
The times you didn't hold your tongue,
The times you failed to curb your cock.

To each of those who've processed me
Into their scrap of fame or pelf:
You think in marks for decency
I'd lose to you? Don't kid yourself.

Averages

The beer is as flat as a pancake, but
The whisky's as strong as a horse.
At the Dog and Duck it's a matter of luck.
And the barman answered "Of course."

The soup is as thick as thieves, but
The fish is as high as a kite.
The stuff you get is simply a bet.
And the waiter replied, "You're right."

The bed is as hard as nails, but
The sex is as good as gold.
"So the odds aren't bad, young feller-me-lad,"
Said the landlord when he was told.

All Things Considered

1. Philosophy Department

Such knotty problems! Check your lists:
How come the universe exists?
How does consciousness, free will,
Match up with brain cells? – Harder still:

Employing what we use for peeing
To penetrate another's being,
And in her complementary hole
Surrendering one's self, one's soul.

Yes, the eternal paradox
Of hearts and minds and cunts and cocks.
That solved, it will be time enough
To tackle all the cosmic stuff.

2. The Logic of Revolution

Ow! A great acorn just fell on my head!
Cut down that oak; plant a upas instead!

3. In the Act

Accepting, at a certain age,
That the world's indeed a stage,
He sees the phonies in the stalls:
For the last time he bellows "Balls!"
    And then the curtain falls.

Vespers

Dusk in St. James's Park, late May:
Soft serenities still play
Round the mossed margins of the lake.
I watch three mallards, one a drake,
Stall skilfully in flight, to drop
Mere inches to a splashdown stop.
Then ... But "Hullo!" – to wreck my mood –
Unreal as ever, there he stood,
No, more unreal, cheeks tighter still
And pallider, eyes yet more chill.
I hadn't seen him for some years,
Had vaguely followed his careers,
Art committees, book prize votes,
Backstabbed colleagues, TV gloats.
His first faint spark had long since gone,
He must have known, but carried on ...
How life had faded from his face!
My answer seemed to meet the case,
"Hullo. I thought that you were dead."
"Well, really, I'm alive," he said.
"In what sense?" He looked aghast.
I watched the landing of one last
Grey goose. And when I turned around
He'd gone. Or sunk into the ground.

Two Exercises in Fiction

1. Well After Kingsley Amis

Her fucking fool of a father
Was waiting when we got home.
He looked as if he had rabies
His face all smothered with foam.

Though I almost at once remembered
This was the old sod's beard,
His high hydrophobic howling
Was worse than the worst we'd feared.

She always said that the reason
Our relationship came to a close
Was that I took the occasion
To give him a punch in the nose.

2. First Sentence of a Novel

The Duchess ran out of the East Wing
Wearing no more than a G-string.

On the Solent

I met her one day on the ferry
That runs to the Isle of Wight,
A girl who appeared to be very
In fact you might almost say quite.

But as it turned out she was barely
In fact you might almost say not:
She left me one day, most unfairly
For a wealthy young man with a yacht.

And as a result I was highly
As I saw their wake streaking the sea
But I said to myself rather wryly
"There'll be more on the mainland for me!"

A Tasting

One should satisfy neither
The emotional heavy breather
Nor the uptight, unsexed
Sniffer of dried text

Half seas over
Or ostentatiously sober
Themes served tartare
Or grilled till they char

Clashing with primary colours
Or nuanced to nothingness
Gross satiation
Or scrawny alienation.

On offer: the homey and wry
Or the slaughterhouse-steamy
Twisted simile-scraps
Or muddled news-clips

Evading coherence
Down a trickle of type-fonts
To sink without closure
In a flatland of posture.

Yes, above all the ones
Who, for whatever reasons
Hype their transcendence
One up on us peasants.

You'll drink to that? Well
Who'll be your clientele?
Only the strange lot
Who don't care what

It says on the label:
But seek deep, indefinable
Savours – much the same
In a wine or a poem.

Through Persepolis

One of those best days:
Everything smiles, satisfies.
Lunch with an editor,
And you'd seldom find brighter;
She's smart, good-looking, we discuss
A great difficult success
We've worked on together,
Over a brisk Sancerre
And a sole meunière ...
And then out past Covent
Garden in an ardent
High autumnal sunshine
Too strong for the Reality
Principle, at least mine.
Yes, bells peal briefly,
But no real trumpets
Sound through gilded streets,
No one really scatters
A richesse of flowers,
And there's no glass coach a-glitter
To hand her into, to lift her,
Now that all's settled and done,
Into the sky, over the sun ...

Quando Dormitant

Among the century's most quoted lines
Are some that don't send shivers up our spines.
Either a good poet, briefly, has foresworn
His talent with indulgence in pure corn
Or, high-prestiged, demanding our respect
Slams down fool's gold and dares us to object.
Examples that your critic designates
Are Auden, Eliot, Lowell, Thomas, Yeats –

"We must love one another or die." Clearly the writer forgot
In the end we must all of us die if we love one another or not.
To do Auden justice, when he went through it
He gave it a questioning look, and then he withdrew it.

"April is the cruellest month." We chose
For that spot, February, when we froze;
Though back indoors we managed, by the fire
To go on mixing memory and desire.

"The lord survives the rainbow of his will"
Rings quite impressively – that is until
Found just as good ripped up and then restored:
"The will survives the rainbow of his lord."
Or, on the Quaker dead a Catholic shrives,
"His rainbow of the will the lord survives."

"Do not go gentle into that good night."
– But if it's good, acceptance should be right,
So perhaps he'd better have reserved his rage
For his discomforts at an earlier stage.

"A terrible beauty is born." – shocked thought
With partisan rhetoric overwrought
– Not used when his own Free State lot
Had seventy-odd republicans shot.

But still, the bards are far less to be blamed
Than those who've kept the public spotlight aimed
Askew. – So amnesty's hereby proclaimed.

Two Translations from Andrei Voznesensky

1. You Live at Your Aunt's

You live at your ballad-studying aunt's.
She sneezes and wears men's underpants.
The damned witch! How we hate her.

We're friends of the barn, like a good bear;
It warms us like hands stuffed in a sweater
And smells of bee-hives.
    And in Suzdal it's Easter!
In Suzdal, there's crowds, laughter, rooks.

You whisper of childhood, as we touch cheeks.
That country childhood, where horses and suns
And honeycombs glitter like icons.
And look at your hair, its honey tints ...

I live in Russia, among snows and saints!

2. Evening on the Building Site

They nag me about 'formalism'.

Experts, at what a distance
You're stuck from life! Formalin:
You stink of it – and incense.

You've got that virgin plain,
But not one pearl of grain ...

Art's dead without a spark
– Human rather than divine –

For bulldozermen to mark
In the taiga's trackless zone;

It comes to them raw and salt
To straighten them up at once,
Unshaven like the sun, pelt
Peeling like bark from pines ...

For some girl of the Chuvashi
Brushing a blue tear away,
Brushing it – sweetly, sluttishly,
Brushing it – like a dragonfly,
To clap hands at rowdily ...

So to me they mean little,
The lances of libel,
The furious label.

Muzak in the Men's Room (Beverly Hills)

Eliminate the Negative
Is more or less appropriate:
But what reaction should I have
To this new (to me) phenomenon
– Camellias too, soft light, gold carpet? ...

Well, why fuss with opinions on
Each oddity life may present?
Don't Fence Me In is the next tune:
Strumming the pink ceramic shine
I hum "no comment" as my comment.

Distancing

The dream recalls: "53864
79, Private Conquest, R.
Is that your name and number?"
"Yes, Sir." "Charged, in the field,
While on active service, that you failed
To ..." what, I don't remember.

Come to that, the things I've failed
To do since then, if they were piled
Up, would make quite a heap.
Why would I dream of that particular
Grey skylight, walls? Just because all so minor?
Dismissed! Get out of my sleep!

Regrets at Being Unable to Attend a Soho Poetry Reading by Mr Scannell

Dear Vernon,
                  When St Anne's sweet chime
Gave notice it was opening time
In we went to drink and rhyme,

Afternoon men come alive
From whatever club or dive
Had seen us through from 3 to 5.

Not *much* more than a pint or two's
Enough: you needn't think the Muse
Floats in on a sea of booze.

In the French Pub the merest pong
Of Pernod swung one into song,
Ripely the evenings rolled along ...

Let's hear it for, and from, you! Cheers!
In Soho after all these years
With high-proof poetry for our ears.

Far and Away

[Epsilon Erídani – so pronounced – the nearest sun-type star then known to have planets]

Philip Larkin (a mind immune
To cant) called the notion that feeling can
Thrive in short lines that rhyme and scan
"Remote as mangoes on the Moon."

A century hence: in Luna City
At Café Larkin a poet drinks
Mango juice fresh from Moonfruit Inc's
Tycho Dome orchard, and says "A pity
That the idea we all can heighten
Our sensibilities by schemes
Of sound and syllable structure seems
Remote as tamarinds on Titan."

After another century: Saturn's
Sky-filling rings, and there beneath
With tamarind-pods for a laurel wreath
A bar-bard mutters "To make word-patterns
Distil a radiance that would rid any
Sub-solar soul of emotional fogs
Seems distant as worlds where they'd serve eggnogs
Out round Epsilon Eridani."

A hundred years later: under Epsilon,
Humanic, high-gened for thoughts and tastes,
A three-point thrummer sits down and wastes
Cooltime with his chattering son,
"A great egg-fruit! Did your off-mate grow it?
The tests that our roboteacher's screened!
– What's a mango? A tamarind?
And one real puzzler – what's a 'poet'?"

Sooner or Later

Changed, when the great equalizer
Has played its black joke,
To a few pounds of fertilizer
Or a few puffs of smoke,

Some ways of such a passing
Strike you sharp and clear:
A van on a zebra crossing,
A vein behind the ear.

Or, with worse scenarios,
A slow melt-down that bores
And exhausts, till dark's victorious,
Not only you, but yours;

You feel the days dismantle
The billion-neuron hoard:
Love sputters like a candle,
Small facts go overboard,

(The mercy speech by Portia,
The words to Gershwin tunes,
The Roman Forts of Yorkshire,
The names of Neptune's moons.)

Anyhow, brain and body,
Here comes a new recruit
To much-missed ranks already
Long since gone down the chute.

What's helpful. Not much. Nothing?
But to fill in the time
There's little harm in clothing
Such nude truths with a rhyme.

IV

Elemental

More swum than the stream
More breathed than the breeze
In all the great scheme
Of things somehow she's

More wholly there
Than their essence could be
More flown than the air
More sailed than the sea

Over and above
What is or occurs
Located by love
On this world of hers.

In Suspense

Mist-murked, a swollen moon protrudes
Out of the West, and brings to mind
– Gibbous, askew – the bare behind
Of one of Stanley Spencer's nudes.

Suet-hued, lax limbs outspread,
Eyes glazed, as if they didn't know
They were being watched: indeed as though
Caught in the dark on infrared.

A dead fly on the canvas web,
Some old cave's supine stalagmite ...
Even this gold-starved, furtive light
Plumbs the pulsed ocean's flow and ebb.

His concepts hardly seem to mesh
Into our more reactive space
– Not just an inexpressive face
But even inexpressive flesh!

Clearly no sex or shock was meant
With genitalia on display
Like organs on a butcher's tray
Quite untransgressive in intent.

With tissue samples cut from time
He sought a fixed, unspurious pose
As truthful as the tightest prose
– Velásquez more like rose-blurred rhyme ...

Moonset: that unorganic sphere
Rolls on; and where we live and breathe
Likewise the sensual spectra seethe
Swept down the irreversible year.

Equatorial

Espèce de soleil! – Laforgue

Sod of a sun! your photon-spew
    Is more than flesh can stand
Your glare sticks in our eyes like glue
    We feel we're breathing sand

Hour by hour you braise or bake
    Our lungs, our throats, our brains
But still our nostrils, though they cake
    Can smell our simmering drains

So smug you hang there overhead
    Time hardly seems to pass
As in our shadeless square you shred
    The dry and desperate grass

How viciously you beat on down
    (It's no excuse that in
St Tropez you gently brown
    Those beachfuls of bare skin)

Downwards at last you start to dip
    You redden, swell and throb
Like the intrusive glans or tip
    Of some huge sky-bloke's knob

Swine of a sun! Still spitting bile
    At last you sink from sight
Good riddance to your flashy style
    Here comes the tasteful night

A breeze, and then in close pursuit
    To soothe our mental burns
The slim moon, cool as she is cute ...
    (But soon the sod returns.)

Offshoots

How can this Apple be defined
By red-green scrapings of its rind?
The sensed blurs with what went before,
Taste, texture, pips and core.
Then, imperfectly, close to sheer
Abstraction, shapes it to a 'sphere',
While, deeper yet, our memories scan
Brush-strokes of Chardin, of Cézanne.

Try 'Water': the slow stream, the pond
Stirred faintly by a flurry of wind
Evoking all that's cool and fresh;
Then vapour-trails; then maelstrom thresh;
Swum seas; tides pouring into verse,
Drenching the pale philosophers.

Just samples of such stimuli
As seethe through every instant. Why?
They ask us, burrowing like moles
Experts on nervous systems, souls ...
But how does that mind-moment meld
With no strange resonance withheld?

As in some bright, tempestuous dawn
All that dazzling detail torn
From sensed, remembered, thought – somehow
Churned up into this single Now.
Such stark asymmetries to blend!
How can the ego apprehend
Its wholeness when that overload
Kicks in, or crack some deeper code?

Behind that bone-curve crowned with hair
The consciousness's rushlights flare
Whose quarter-million hours awake
Stir memories that blur and break,
Half-worn tapestries woven of
Old colour-chords of loss or love.

So best shun any master scheme.
Eat that apple, cross that stream,
Chewing one's best to neutralise
Nude Aphrodite's golden prize.
There'll be no naiads in that rill
So let's forget about them. (Still ...)

Nocturne

"Broad Daylight" – words you speak or write
Imputing narrowness to Night?

•

Night's only moonlit, starlit, yet
See from that delicate palette
The crested wave that brims the cove
The breeze-blown-blossomed apple grove.

•

Even when deepest dark has spread,
The lovers on the unlit bed,
In a deep sensuousness embraced,
Enjoy touch, hearing, scent and taste:
All the senses except sight
Providing adequate delight.
– While outside, champion of the dark,
The nightingale outsings the lark.

•

That sweet bird's spectrum? Perhaps instead
Of Day's " ... green, yellow, orange, red"
She, other creatures of the Night
Take in "... frost, steel, silver, white"
For all we know, these are no less
Compelling to their consciousness
As rich on their subjective screens
As all our diverse reds and greens.

•

And then, look up! The clear Night is
Home to all deeps and distances
Where ritualled constellations reign
Like some scored musical refrain,
Voids vivid there with planets, stars,
Diamond Vega, vermilion Mars,
The pale mesh of the Milky Way,
The meteor-shower's high, silent spray.

•

– Just match their breadths and depths and heights.
Night's limit to our naked sight's
That faintest blur M 31
In Andromeda, two million
Light-years! – Rather different from
Day's ten light-minutes maximum!
In fact Day's narrow limits are
Mere suburbs of one G-type star.

•

How would humans be if they
Were strictly creatures of the Day?
Asleep at dusk, up after dawn,
Night's treasures would have stayed unknown,
Those vistaed vaults would not have brought
Awed feelings, challenges to thought.

•

"Broad Daylight"'s commonly the time
Allotted to some loathsome crime
But let's concede, more cause for fright
Lurks in the narrower "Dead of Night".

Extrapolation

The thin crescent to the West:
Lit outline of a single breast
Of a sky-goddess otherwise
Wholly in shadow, and the size
Of half-a-dozen constellations ...
Our imagery's impatience
Distorts the real sky
– But closer, and equally
Part of the universe,
There are such shapes as hers.

Grace Notes

The embarrassment of
Childish words of love,
'Blossom queen', 'honey dove'.

When girls (an old sage said)
Strip for a man's bed
Shame too should be shed.

And now? – As words get
More infantile yet:
'Baby lamb', 'angel pet'.

Reconnaissance

On a clear night, we may look up at the All
As if standing at the central
Point of a huge flash-freaked black opal.

Then, past our vision, the mind supplies
Metagalaxies, immensities
For those impressible by mere size,

Well, we're nearing technologies that could scan
Cities on planets of Aldebaran,
Oceans as far off as M 31.

– And the forward edge of the far future's
Wave'll sweep right over those frontiers
For our heirs' almost endless voyages and ventures.

'Almost' because the very universe
Must in the end darken and disperse
Or so say our current cosmographers.

They plumb near the Big Bang's first nanosecond
– Though that may be only scraping the rind
If the full fruit's forever beyond.

2

We've always trolled for implicit patterns.
Lucretius interwove a sleet of atoms.
Some Greeks stamped number on reality's phantoms.

Random stars fell into constellations
Imposed on the celestial regions
By the ancient craving for aggregations

And, centuries later, the Hereford Map
Gave the world strict, but spurious, shape:
Jerusalem at the centre, a mental warp.

Now: seething quanta, dimensions, a spate
Of force-fields round which intricate
Equations weave their dazzling net.

But unobserved arrhythmias thresh
Around and soon break out of the mesh.
The massive computing starts afresh

And, as the phenomena froth and foam,
From our polders we toil to divert and dam
The oceans of the continuum.

3

William James once wrote of how temperament
Determined each philosopher's bent.
With the data so weak, we can only assent.

Though surely only the most rigid doctrine
Solely depends on (say) the endocrine
Balance or what's in the brain-dead groin?

There are, of course, many scenarios,
Quite a collector's cellar of curios.
We can only go where our thoughts will carry us,

Which mayn't be far – the point's Robert Heinlein's –
Any more than a collie has much of a chance
To grasp how its dog food gets into cans.

4

Some ache for those worlds beyond the voids
With appropriate orbits, the needed fluids,
To commune with minds of non-anthropoids.

But, above all, there's the heavy artillery
Of instruments, the tempestuous flurry
Of equations tearing through thickets of theory

And why shouldn't sages with minds like prisms
Probe the intergalactic chasms
Enjoying their new-knowledge orgasms?

Still, tracking the trail of the Big Bang
Is a waste for those happy with Yin and Yang
Or leaning back into the Allfühlung.

5

If to peter out is the lot of the All
Its tenure is longer than ours, but still
We may find some sort of parallel.

As wavelengths flatten to infinite
(Or are crushed to minima less than nought)
Existence fades into total night.

Meanwhile minds bred up from matter
– At once their prey and their predator –
Are faced with various ultimata.

Of the whole, we've only the thinnest slice
Just a brief tangle till we're torn loose
From the thorns of time, the weeds of space.

Does that last wrench, as the body-link goes
Or almost so, fill a timeless pause
Where the unflake falls and the unstream flows?

6

Research-hounds, trained to be untranscendental,
In two different packs hot on the scent will
Flush out the mood-modes, material, mental.

Some trace the intense billion neuron torque
That the crimped folds of the cortex spark;
Others strip the viewed psyche stark.

But concept-cantilevers somehow don't solve
The bridging of the spidery gulf
Between the nerved senses and the self.

7

Half-free of the clumsy cosmos-grope,
As if not quite woken from non-REM sleep,
Wisps of totality may take shape,

Mist moments smooth as chiselled stone,
Sweet Agnosis, sculptor Anon,
With all of the undivine withdrawn,

And, faintly felt through the near-alive,
The softest touch of a tendril of love
Too light for leaf or belief ...

The Fells (mid-19th C)

Fuzzy white cords of snow intertwine, trailing
Down from humped cloud-mass across his eyes:
A low light jostles unsteadily through
Ripped rags of the West horizon – paling

Backdrop to regretted decision.
Feet, mind trudge on between barbed hedges,
Numb fields. Boughs hang soggy black, any green
Trace supplied more by memory than vision.

No real colour, then. No reds or pinks
No holly-berry, flicker of robin-breast.
A fatigued yellow only, from the windows ahead.
But flakes feather about him. He huddles his senses. And thinks,

As he plods on to the place where he shouldn't go,
That after all the world could be worse. For at least
The spinning dark in the depths of the cumulus
Doesn't weave black snow.

Last Hours

The coast cools down the afternoon
And slowly a sky the colour of corn
Peels away round a reddening sun.

That creamy monotone dispersed,
Lime and umber, roan and rust
Well up out of the ored West.

Old vaults polish extreme song,
Intense vintage is smooth on the tongue,
The mind warms to the subtle and strong;

And pressed out of a dying sky
Sweeps of coloured profundity
Fill the heart as they fill the eye.

Sophocles and others, so we're taught,
Showed old age gather such glow of thought
To plenitude. Was it still too short?

Over this dim broadness of bay,
Pale tuberose, crimson ray
Brim over, and start to seep away.

The great sunset loses its strength.
The cloud's black that was hyacinth.
(Sophocles crumbles on his plinth) ...

The thick hues, the transparencies:
It all devolves into a darkness,
Folds back into the cool abyss.

Dead in the water, the day is done.
There's nothing new under the sun,
Still less when it's gone down.

Black Sea

Lynx-lithe, a concentrate of light
Swoops, sudden, through the headland firs,
Claws slashing the soft lens of sight.
Even the thewed slope shakes and blurs.

The sun's outflanked the earlier shade
Of foliage with a horizontal
Blaze. Half-blind, we turn and wade
Through photon-seethe to our hotel

But soon we're over the effects
Of the harsh cosmos breaking through.
Fish from the bay, dry wine, sweet sex,
Then the veranda, whence we view

For now, a dimmer, different world
That wildness tamed; – while over there
The ground beneath the trees lies curled
Up like a hibernating bear.

Chalet

The wild wind, the white wind ...

Inside, in their long weekend,
Perhaps their last,
There seems no season
Only exhausted obsession
With their past,
Like a film in color
Perversely techniqued to black-and-white,
Their unfeeling set in the pallor
Of a stiff glaze.
                – But now
Suddenly, a frenzy of love-hate ...

The wolf-wind howls through the snow ...

Index of Titles and First Lines

A Note About the Author

Robert Conquest was born in Malvern, Worcestershire, in 1917, to an American father and his English wife. Educated at Winchester College, the University of Grenoble, and Magdalen College, Oxford, he took his B.A. and (later) M.A. degrees in politics, philosophy, and economics, and his D. Litt. in Soviet history.

In Lisbon on an American passport at the outbreak of the Second World War, he returned to England to serve in the Oxfordshire and Buckinghamshire Light Infantry, and in 1944 was sent from Italy on Balkan military missions awkwardly attached to the Soviet Third Ukrainian Front – and later the Allied Control Commission in Bulgaria. From 1946 to 1956, he worked in the British Foreign Service – first in Sofia, then in London, and in the U.K. Delegation to the United Nations – after which he varied periods of freelance writing with academic appointments.

Conquest's poems were published in various periodicals from 1937. In 1945 the PEN Brazil Prize for a war poem was awarded to his "For the Death of a Poet" – about an army friend, the poet Drummond Allison, killed in Italy (published in *The Book of the PEN 1950*) – and in 1951 he received a Festival of Britain verse prize. Since then he has brought out six volumes of poetry previous to *Penultimata*, and one of literary criticism (*The Abomination of Moab*). He has published a verse translation of Aleksandr Solzhenitsyn's epic *Prussian Nights* (1977), and two novels, *A World of Difference* (1955), and (with Kingsley Amis) *The Egyptologists* (1965). In 1955 and 1963 Conquest edited the influential *New Lines* anthologies, and in 1962-1963 he was literary editor of the *London Spectator*.

He is the author of twenty-one books on Soviet history, political philosophy, and international affairs, the most recent being *The Dragons of Expectation* (2004). His classic, *The Great Terror*, has appeared in most European languages, as well as in Japanese, Arabic, Hebrew and Turkish.

In 1959-60 he was Visiting Poet and Lecturer in English at the University of Buffalo, and has also held research appointments at the London School of Economics, the Columbia University Russian Institute, the Woodrow Wilson International Center for Scholars, the Heritage Foundation, and Harvard University's Ukrainian Research Institute.

In 1990 he presented Granada Television's *Red Empire*, a seven-part documentary on the Soviet Union which was broadcast in the UK, the USA, and in various other countries, including Australia and Russia.

Conquest is a Fellow of the Royal Society of Literature, the British Academy, the American Academy of Arts and Sciences, and the British Interplanetary Society, and is also a member of the Society for the Promotion of Roman Studies (contributing to *Britannia* an article on the Roman Place Names of Scotland). His honours and awards include the Order of the British Empire and Companion of the Order of St. Michael and St. George; the Jefferson Lectureship (1993); the American Academy of Arts and Letters' Michael Braude Award for Light Verse (1997); the Richard Weaver Award for Scholarly Letters (1999); the Fondazione *Liberal* Career Award (2004); and the Presidential Medal of Freedom (2005).

He and his wife Elizabeth live in California, where he has long worked as a research fellow at Stanford University's Hoover Institution.